A Fresh Wave Of Marketing

An Intentional Approach To Marketing For
Visionary CEOs

Casey Gromer

Clara Gromer, Age 8

This book is dedicated to my daughter, Clara, who is my inspiration for being more intentional at work so I am able to experience the other joys in my life.

"The visionary starts with a clean sheet of paper, and re-imagines the world."
~Malcom Gladwell

Preface

"What really draws me to this business is the power we have, as marketers, to change the World."
~Casey Gromer, Virtual Marketing Officer

Never have I heard someone say, "I want to work so much that I never see my kids or my spouse or my friends again." No one starts a business intending to give up all the things they enjoy in life.

But that's exactly what happened to me. I spent 15 years leading marketing teams for Corporate America, and while I loved the work and loved the people, I lost ME.

I led high stress projects and was on-call 24/7. I was constantly on my phone, working through lunch and dinner, and passing up activities with people I loved. In the midst of this high stress work, I started my family. As an "older mom" (I was 34 when my first babe was born), I knew I couldn't keep up this pace and still be the parent my child needed.

So I gave up my cushy, low-risk corporate job to go into business for myself as a marketing consultant. I was still doing the same work, still supporting the same Fortune 50 clients, but making a LOT more money. On the surface, it sounded fab!

Fast forward another two kids....

And then I got sick. The constant stress and anxiety took a toll on my body. I contracted Lyme disease. After an aggressive treatment protocol, I had rid myself of those nasty bugs. But I suffered a myriad of other chronic health issues as a result of my weakened immune system and inflamed body.

My health went downhill from there. Standard Western medicine doctors couldn't figure out what was wrong. They offered little in the way of diagnosing me and even less in terms of helping me feel better.

In order to heal, I took my health into my own hands. I studied everything health related I could get my hands on. I read books, downloaded research papers, followed blogs, and listened to podcasts. Eventually, as a last resort, I booked an appointment with a naturopathic doctor. Her perspective on treating the whole body rather than chasing individual symptoms was refreshing. I appreciated this approach so much that I added a functional medicine practitioner to my team of health professionals.

This entire experience opened my eyes to better ways of living. I began to understand the impact of what we put in and on our bodies, how we shape our minds, and how we treat our environment.

After re-assessing my priorities, I became more intentional with both my personal and my business life. And as such, I was able to focus on my health and well-being. I'm a better parent, a better marketer, and a stronger business owner for it.

Today, my family and I are living our dream on a small lake in central Minnesota. We wake up each morning to the beauty of Mother Nature. And we have all become more intentional about how we spend and prioritize our time.

I completely relaunched my consulting business — Casey Gromer VMO — for the visionary with dreams of making this world a better place. I want to help you be more intentional about your own dreams by stepping out of the implementer role and into the CEO role. Let's get all those day-to-day details off your plate so you can be intentional about YOUR priorities, just like I did.

As a partner in your business, I take marketing completely off your plate. I set up your systems and processes, manage your team, and make sure no balls get dropped in the day-to-day of creating visibility and excellent experiences for you most prized possession — your customers.

I am your marketing Chief Of Staff. And I support you in your role of CEO without the burnout, late nights, cancelled dates, missed activities, high stress, and health issues.

It's time for a Fresh Wave of Marketing.

Are you ready to get out of the day-to-day and step into your role as CEO?

Table Of Contents

Introduction

Let's imagine for a minute that you are living the dream.

You spent years scheming of how to turn your passion into a business. You're a true visionary. You have big dreams and goals that you know will change the world.

Every day, you wake up excited to go to work. You're excited for the possibilities the day will bring, for the work you'll be accomplishing, the people you'll impact, the connections you'll make, and the relationships you'll nurture.

And after your perfect day of changing the world at work, you'll come home and kiss your spouse and hug your kids hello. You'll all be singing kumbaya around the dinner table that was lovingly home cooked. You're looking forward to some quiet time with the love of your life on the couch after the kids go to bed and whipping up some fun weekend plans.

Isn't it grand to be an entrepreneur?

Except for most of us, this is not the reality.

Our reality is fraught with hasty decisions, financial stress, overwork, miscommunication, and utter chaos.

Our teams are depending on us to lead and inspire, but instead we are buried in the day-to-day aspects of running the business.

Where did that passion go? And when was it replaced with burnout?

But it doesn't have to be that way.

If you want to step into your role as visionary and CEO, you've got to start thinking like a CEO.

But what does that even mean?

Regardless of the current size of your business or your long-term revenue goals, there are certain things that successful CEOs start doing early on and continue throughout their leadership role. Think of these activities as "growth mindset" for business.

So, if your business vision includes growth, then there are 4 basic activities that you can implement in your business RIGHT NOW to set yourself up to achieve your goals.

4 THINGS SUCCESSFUL BUSINESSES DO ON THE REGULAR TO ACHIEVE GROWTH

1. Think Strategically.

While there is more to business strategy than thinking strategically, the idea is that strategy isn't a once and done activity.

Your business and marketing strategy is the foundation of your success. It's what drives your decisions, keeps your team focused, and tracks and measures your success.

It's an outdated thought process that only businesses applying for financing or venture capital need a written business plan.

Your customers are inundated on a daily basis by competing messages and offers. Without a strong foundation - your strategy - your teams will lack focus, your goals won't be aligned, and your message will get lost in a sea of noise.

Successful businesses have a thoughtful business and marketing strategy. They write it down. They share their strategy with their teams so everyone feels invested in their success. They revisit their strategy on a regular basis — tweaking, clarifying, updating, and tracking.

2. Plan.

Strategy is important. It's foundational. But it's the ability to create a plan of action once you've defined your strategy that gets results.

Planning falls into two types: long-term planning and short-term planning.

Long-term plans focus on where you're heading, major goals, and milestones. Many businesses like to set major milestones out 1 year, 5 years, or even 10 years in advance.

Short-term plans focus on how you'll get there. Ninety-day action plans are a popular way to focus on smaller, shorter-term goals. This allows businesses to be more focused and flexible by planning and implementing in "sprints." It's easier to review your results and apply tweaks.

The key to success with short-term planning is being able to tie your short-term goals back to the long-term objectives you've identified in your vision.

3. Improve Continually.

The old adage, "if it ain't broke, don't fix it," works well if you are a business who's happy to stay stagnant. But, what's working today isn't guaranteed to work tomorrow as the world around us changes at breakneck speed.

To compete, you must continuously be looking for new and better ways of doing things. How can you make your products, services, and processes better? How can you be more efficient? How can you become more educated about your industry, your business, your self?

Being consistent and intentional about continuous improvement results in greater customer satisfaction, reduced costs, and improved margins.

4. Invest In People.

People are paramount to the success of your business. Without quality people, your business is going nowhere.

You can invest in people either by hiring and handing off pieces of your business or by investing in the people who have already joined you in your venture.

Business owners that shy away from the risk of hiring help or who struggle to hand off pieces of their business will never grow. You can't keep pouring into a full cup and expect it not to overflow. Investing in the right help not only frees up your time so you can focus on other aspects of growing your business, but if done correctly, it allows you to bring in experts in areas that aren't your strength. Build a skilled leadership team and trust them with pieces of your business that make you stronger and more efficient — freeing you up to focus on what's really important. As CEO, your focus should be inspiring your team, generating ideas, closing big deals, building relationships, and solving the tough problems.

What does this look like?

Investing in your existing support team also has positive benefits for the growth of your business. Whether you encourage training and education, self-development, team building, or community service, any time you invest time or money into the people who serve you, you build rapport and relationships that encourage most of your staff to continue doing their best work for you.

How do you stack up? Where are you spending your time and what shifts can you make in the way you approach your business to set you up for continued growth?

How to use
this book

For the purposes of this book, we will focus on creating and maintaining a cohesive marketing strategy. Then we will develop the systems and processes necessary to execute.

A solid strategy is the foundation from which the other activities in your business are built.

You strategy drives what initiatives go into your plan. It communicates your vision and direction to your team so they can better support you.

Systems and processes provide a roadmap for your team to not only support your vision, but to plan and execute on it. Marketing systems should be repeatable and scalable — meaning they can be used over and over again and they grow with you as your business expands.

The philosophies and principles in this book are based largely off the *Entrepreneurial Operating System* (EOS®) founded by Gino Wickman. The Entrepreneurial Operating System is a set of systems and tools designed to help entrepreneurs develop healthy, functional leadership teams, get employees on the same page with the company vision, and create systems for efficient execution.

For the purposes of this book, we will focus on building the marketing segment of your leadership team.

This book is the perfect tool to use in conjunction with the Marketing Growth Formula program (www. MarketingGrowthFormula.com). If you aren't following along with the program, you can use this book to guide you in developing your 6 pillars of strategy, setting up your planning systems, and managing the work. Your ultimate goal after completing this book is to be comfortable enough with your strategy and planning systems to hand your marketing off to a trusted expert so you can get out of the day-to-day and still be confident that your business is spending time and money doing the right things to move the needle forward.

Before we begin, your first lesson is that all things in your business need to be documented. To make things easy, we've created a simple template you can download to keep track of your marketing strategy as you move through the chapters of this book.

To access your template, go to http://bit.ly/MarketingGrowthTemplate. You will need to make a copy of the template and save it as your own.

Set a goal to spend roughly 1 week on each pillar. This gives you an opportunity to digest the information, think about how that pillar operates within your business, research and discuss with members of your team, and document it.

Schedule weekly meetings with your leadership team to brainstorm each pillar, or invite your most trusted team members to the conversation. Involving other people in your discussion not only gives you different perspectives to consider, but also helps team members feel more engaged and improves employee satisfaction.

This book is short. And while it's a quick read, it's intended to initiate ACTION. Use each chapter as an opportunity to take action by reviewing and discussing each topic in depth.

The chapter topics are:

- Know Your WHY
- How To Attract Your TRIBE
- Know Your AUDIENCE
- VALIDATE Your Idea
- How To STAND OUT
- Solve Your Customers PROBLEM
- Know Your NUMBERS
- Your Marketing in ACTION

OTHER TIPS FOR USING THIS WORKBOOK —

Throw perfectionism out the window. Yes, your strategy is critical to paving your path to success. But making it perfect will never happen. Be comfortable knowing when your best is good enough.

If you get stuck, move on. Often times we find ourselves with a bit of "writer's block," so to speak. If the answer is just not coming to you right away, know that the elements of your plan are interconnected. So as you move on and make decisions on other parts of of your strategy, it might become crystal clear when you go back to those pieces that have you stumped.

Do not write with pen. Okay, not literally. But my point is that your strategy is never intended to be etched in stone. As your business evolves and the market changes, so might pieces of your strategy. And that's okay. Google Maps didn't get it perfect on the first try either.

Tread carefully when seeking input. Feedback is one of the single most helpful tools to making business decisions....when it comes from the right people. If you need to bounce ideas off of others, make sure they know your business and your customers. Otherwise, you might end up chasing a bunch of well-intentioned suggestions that are not relevant to your business.

Have no expectations. Laying your foundation could take anywhere from a couple of days to a couple of months. How long it takes you to craft your strategy depends on how precise you want to be, the type industry you're in, and the size of your business, among other factors. And any amount of strategic planning you do is still going to provide value to your business in terms of defining how you spend your time and money to be successful.

Each chapter includes:

- An "assignment"
- An educational component to help you understand the importance and relevance of each strategic component
- Tips and examples on how to apply that strategic component to your business

Let's get started.

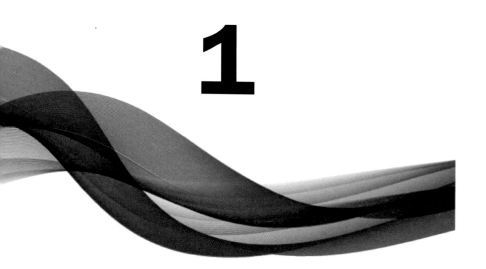

1

Know Your WHY

Once upon a time, eons ago, I joined a network marketing company because...well, because everyone was doing it. And I wanted to be cool, too.

At first, I was pretty excited about the venture. I loved the products and I shared about them whenever I got a chance. I enjoyed my discounts. But after a bit, my excitement fizzled. And once my cabinets were bursting at the seams with all the product I was saving so much money on, I ran out of more things to buy.

My friends and family were getting annoyed at hearing about my latest "amazing" product that would miraculously change their lives.

And I dropped out.

This scenario might sound familiar to you. Unless you've been living under a rock, you have most likely either met someone in network marketing or perhaps you even joined a network marketing company for yourself for the same reasons I did.

It might not surprise you to hear that the success rate on network marketing businesses is not that great. According to a study conducted by Jon M. Taylor, within the first year, at least 50% of the people who sign up with network marketing companies drop out. And within 5 years, at least 90% have given up.

There are various reasons why the network marketing model doesn't work for most people. But the one that stuck out to me was the lack of a purpose-driven "why."

According to Simon Sinek in his bestseller "It Starts With Why," people don't buy WHAT you do, they buy WHY you do it.

Many of the businesses that come to me already have a purpose. But their purpose is so short sighted, that it fails to inspire anyone — even themselves.

In the case of network marketing, you might hear many of the successful sellers claim that they are making millions without lifting a finger. Or that they are supporting their family, their $1mm home and their multiple trips to the Bahamas while only working 5 hours a week.

Sounds amazing, right? These stories attract the attention of many. But I'll let you in on a little secret.

Money is not enough.

While the lure of easy money might sound like a dream come true, most people find that it's not enough to inspire them to work hard enough to get to that place of making a comfortable income while hardly lifting a finger.

So in this chapter, we will work on defining your "why." Or if you already have a purpose, I challenge you to question whether that purpose is big enough to inspire you and those around you to success.

Vision

Of all the exercises in this entire book, the visioning exercise is by far my favorite. But that never used to be the case.

Back in graduate school, I wrote many vision statements. They were bland and boring.

"... In <insert time frame>, <Name of company> will <insert an achievement that involves what you do> by <insert the unique way in which you will accomplish this>."

Blah, blah, blah.

Insert your company's vision into this statement. Does it inspire you? It's probably not that inspirational. And if you look at your competitors, chances are their vision statements look very similar.

So how, then, do we break this mold of cookie cutter visions and turn our thoughts towards more meaningful and inspirational purpose?

First, let's explore the basic function of a vision statement.

Your vision is a tool used to communicate your company's purpose and long-term goals to stakeholders.

You will create a vision statement and use it as a reminder for **where you are headed**. It will help you set your goals, create your plans, and communicate with customers, team members and services who work for you or on your behalf.

Here are some basic tips for tackling your vision:

- Gather your stakeholders. Your vision should not be created in a vacuum. Getting input from your leadership team is a key component of creating a solid vision your entire company can get behind.
- Keep it simple. Your vision is not a catchy phrase you'll be making public.
- Keep it short and succinct. Your vision needs to be something engrained in the back of your mind as you go about your day to day. One to two sentences should be enough.
- Visualize your business in 5-10 years. Use your vision to describe what you see.
- Consider your "why." Why are you in business?

By the technical definition of visions statement, we could stop right there and call it good.

But I know you wouldn't be here if you wanted a bland, cookie-cutter business.

The reason the visioning exercise is my favorite is because I open my clients' eyes to the possibilities of purpose that are right in front of their face, but they struggle to articulate. You can literally see the blanket of limiting beliefs slowly drop from over their face as they envision the new world where they are a catalyst to change.

Here are some ways you can dig deeper to find the underlying purpose for all your hard work:

- First, make sure the vision is not about you. Make it about something bigger—bigger than what you can comfortably imagine. If your vision talks about how big you will grow or how much revenue you will make, keep digging.
- What change are you inspiring? And what does the world look like if you are successful?
- Consider your company values. Whatever you strongly believe should be woven into your vision statement.
- Don't focus on what you sell. What you sell is just a vehicle for achieving your goals.

For inspiration, check out some sample vision statements from some of your favorite companies.

"Our vision is to be earth's most customer-centric company; to build a place where people can come to find and discover anything they might want to buy online."
~Amazon

"Be THE destination for customers to save money, no matter how they want to shop."
    ~Wal-Mart

"...to accelerate the world's transition to sustainable energy."
    ~Tesla

Now you try it. Pull up your Marketing Growth Formula template and play around with your vision statement.

Having a solid vision statement doesn't necessarily make you instantly inspirational. In the network marketing company I joined, for example, I actually believed in the cause of the company I supported. But after roughly a year into the relationship, I felt the lines of purpose blur. The message from leadership was being distilled on the way down through multiple levels of consultants — all with their own versions of "why." And what began as a message to "change the world" turned into "buy more product" and "spend more money" by the time it reached the feet on the street.

Mission

As Simon Sinek says, if you know your "why," it makes it much easier to figure out the "how."

And if your vision statement defines where you are going, then your mission statement is how you'll get there.

Your mission statement outlines the framework for how you move your business forward in achieving your vision. It is your core focus. Your mission helps you stay in your own lane so you aren't distracted by things that don't align.

It can be confusing to try to narrow everything you are about into one single statement. But a mission statement is the ultimate form of clarity and focus — two of my major mantras in running a successful business.

Successful businesses find their one thing and focus on doing it better than anyone else. Your mission is your "one thing."

Here are some basic tips for tackling your mission:

- **Don't stress.** Again, perfectionism will not get you progress. You should be comfortable with your mission statement. It should make you feel good. But finding the perfect words is not necessary — unless your mission statement is a visible component of your marketing.
- **The shorter the better.** One to five sentences should be enough to convey what you need.
- **Do not Google.** While it may be okay to look for examples of great mission statements to inspire you, make sure you aren't copying. Remember, this mission statement is what drives YOUR business. It needs to be unique to you.
  Ask yourself:
  - What do I do?
  - How do I do it?
  - Who do I do it for?
  - Why do I do it (what value do I add)?
- **Align your mission statement to your vision.**

You will know when you have a successful mission statement when your customers can read it and know, without a doubt, that it's you. If your mission statement could pass for any of your competitors' businesses, then go back to the drawing board until you've focused on your "one thing."

Want to take your mission statement to the next level?

When you write your mission statement, make it specific and actionable. Your employees and stakeholders should be held accountable to whatever is contained in your mission statement.

For example, instead of "world class customer service," use "will respond to every customer inquiry."

Your mission statement is the place for you to articulate what you do. What services or products do you provide that show the world how you will achieve your "why?"

If creative writing isn't your strength, you can use this simple exercise to help you brainstorm your mission statement — as long as you apply the above principles to the phrases you insert.

Complete this phrase: <Company> mission is <insert what you do> for <insert who you do it for> by <how or why you do it>.

Take a look at how this mission supports the previous vision.

Now you try it. Pull up your Marketing Growth Formula template and play around with your mission statement. Don't forget to hit "save!"

Goal Setting

Goals are the mechanism business owners use to define what success look like.

In your vision, you laid out a passionate "why" to inspire your customers and your team to join you on the journey. But how will you know once you've achieved that vision?

Goals define what your vision looks like using specific, measurable criteria that draws a line in the sand for you. Once you reach that line, you'll know you've arrived.

And, if you have meaningful and appropriate goals set for your business, they serve as a guide for implementing the other elements of your strategy.

According to Amazon, there are 4,800 books on goal setting at our disposal. I've probably read half of them. Lucky for you, we are going to break it down to a quick, easy process.

Goal setting can be used in lots of different ways. For the purposes of this book, you are going look out 3-5 years to create some long-term goals that define what your world looks like once you've achieved your vision.
Tips for tackling your long-term goals:

I'm sure you've heard of the acronym "S.M.A.R.T." But just in case, here's a refresher.

- Set SPECIFIC goals. A specific goal will identify who is involved, what is getting accomplished, and a timeline for when it will be done. Also consider location (if it's relevant).
- Goals must be MEASURABLE. At any time along your journey, you should be able to measure how far you've come towards achieving them.
- Be sure your goals are actually ACHIEVABLE. It's a good idea to think big and be optimistic about your abilities. But setting goals too far outside your realm of reality is actually setting you up to fail.

- Similarly, be REALISTIC. You need to be both willing AND able to do what it takes to reach your goals. Is it the right time? Is it the right fit? Is the effort worth it?
- Lastly, make it TIMELY. Set a date. For this piece of our marketing strategy, we are looking out 1, 3, and 5 years.

Before I have you dive into setting your own goals, I'd like to give you an eagle's eye view of how I approach goal setting for my clients.

3-5 YEAR STRATEGIC GOALS

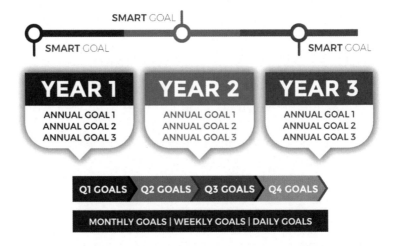

In short, the goals you set for you business for the next 3-5 years will drive the activity you plan for your business annually, quarterly, and weekly. We'll talk more about what this looks like in chapter 7.

What are your top three to five business goals for the next few years? Go to your Marketing Growth Formula template and write them out.

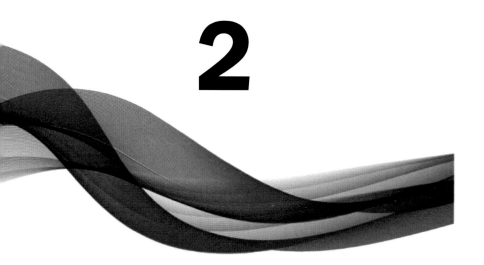

2

Attract your TRIBE

Have you heard the saying, "Your vibe attracts your tribe?" Science says that it's 100% true.

The "vibe" we put out — our mental and emotional energy — is how we communicate to others. We are constantly putting out vibes, either consciously or subconsciously, looking for others who share our same frequency.

It is human nature to want to "belong." People are desperately searching out groups and individuals who "get it" — who they can relate to. They want to feel validated. They are searching for a tribe because there is comfort and joy in feeling understood and included.

As businesses, this same principle applies. We need to be intentional about the vibe we are putting into the marketing place so that we attract the people who are most likely to want what we have to offer and buy from us. In the business world, our "vibe" is also called our brand.

Contrary to popular belief, your brand is much more than your logo and visuals.

Your brand is how people perceive you in the marketplace. It's what goes through their minds whenever they interact with you.

Every touch your audience has with your business affects how they perceive you. Whether it's on social media, through customer service, an in-person experience, or a paid ad, your brand is giving off vibes and making a lasting impact on the minds of your customer.

The key to a strong brand is consistency. The way you show up across all your platforms, the way you serve your customers, the way you communicate with your audience needs to be consistent. People need to feel comfortable that they know what they're going to get when they connect with you.

People don't always buy rationally. So think about the emotion that your brand conveys. And don't forget to be authentic. Authenticity goes a long way to establishing trust.

Are you prepared to be the thought leader behind your brand?

Brand Story

Your brand story paints a picture of a journey for your audience. Whether it's your personal journey or a journey you envision for your customers, your brand story provides a way for your customers to emotionally connect and relate to you.

Your brand story pulls your customers into your "why." Why do you do what you do? On what journey are you taking them?

Your brand story might paint a picture of a problem, follow the journey to resolution, and describe what life looks like after success.

In your marketing strategy template:

- Define the problem
- Describe the journey
- Deliver the solution
- Create an image of what success looks like

It's really important that your brand story is authentic. You don't need to have an overly dramatic or impressive brand story to make an impact. You just need it to be true, realistic, and meaningful. Most people find it easier to connect to stories that are relatable. And most can smell a fake story from a mile away. Sometimes it's not the story itself that your customers remember, but the way you tell it.

The perspective from which you tell your story is also important. Put yourself in your customer's shoes. The best and most successful marketers (and CEOs) have the ability to see life through their customer's eyes. Your brand story is no different. The more we ask ourselves "why do they care," the better our story becomes and the deeper the connection we make.

Writing our brand story can be freeing! Many visionaries struggle to put their "why" into words. Once they are able to see their brand story told in a meaningful way, they can't wait to share it with their audience. So they will create a single marketing piece, send out a single communication, or update their website — and never visit their brand story again.

Your brand story isn't just about the words on your "About" page or the copy in your company brochure. Your brand story is a foundational piece of your message that you weave into daily interactions with your audience and customers in an authentic way.

You don't necessarily need to tell your entire brand story each time you communicate with your audience, but you need to make sure the things you communicate — the WAY you communicate — is in line with your brand story. That consistency, over time, is what connects you to your customers on a more emotional level.

Brand Personality

It's much easier for people to connect with other humans than it is for them to connect with a company. Companies are big, overwhelming, and intangible. So, to make your business more relatable to your customers, you need to "humanize" your brand.

Humanizing your brand is the process of giving your business human-like traits that help customers relate to you on a deeper level.

The humanization of a brand is what is referred to as brand personality.

Brand personality makes it easy for audiences to form an emotional attachment. It's how you'll present yourself to your audience and how you'll respond and interact. It creates consistency and cohesiveness across the different channels you use to connect with customers, prospects, and stakeholders.

Consider your brand personality the chance to impact how people think, feel, and react when they come in contact with your business. Your brand personality gives customers confidence that they'll have the same experience every time they engage with your business.

People are more likely to be drawn to a brand that either contains traits that are of high value to them or traits that mirror their own personality. They want to be able to see themselves in your brand. So it's important that you define and use your brand personality in a way that resonates with your audience, but also reflects your vision and values.

Use this list of potential personality traits to help you consider your own brand personality.

- Adventurous
- Charming
- Confident
- Conscientious
- Cultured
- Dependable
- Encouraging
- Intelligent
- Observant
- Optimistic
- Exuberant
- Fair
- Fearless
- Helpful
- Humble
- Imaginative
- Independent
- Persistent
- Reliable
- Trusting

Think about how you want people to think and feel about you. Once you have decided which personality traits best represent your company, go ahead and document them in your strategy template. Be careful not to pick too many. It can water down your message and make it confusing to your audience. I suggest sticking to no more than 3 solid traits that can really shine in your marketing.

Brand Values

In our personal lives, values are the ideals that we hold most important. Values determine our priorities and help us measure our achievements.

In his book, "The Subtle Art Of Not Giving A F*ck," Mark Manson states:

*"The key to living a good life is not giving a f*ck about more things but rather to focus only on the things that align with your personal values."*

Basically, what Mark is saying (in a rather crude way) is that if you focus your energy on too many things, you will never be able to impact anything. You will be stretched thin, burnt out, and ultimately unhappy.

The same is true for your business.

By focusing your business on the things that are the most important — the values that align with your mission and vision — you are able to focus yourself and your teams on the things that will really drive your vision forward.

In business, your brand values serve two purposes:

1. Your brand values serve as your compass. They help you determine your direction. Ultimately, you will make decisions in your business based on your values.

2. Your brand values will attract an audience of people with the same or similar values.

Your core brand values are unique to you — like a fingerprint. A strong set of values will differentiate you from other similar businesses in your market.

When I'm working with clients to help them define their core values, I ask them to think about their soap boxes. What are the things your business believes in so strongly that you could stand up on a stage and preach about to anyone who would listen?

Let's consider brand values of some of the heavy hitters. Google operates under the following set of core values:

- Focus on the user and all else will follow.
- It's best to do one thing really, really well.
- Fast is better than slow.
- Democracy on the web works.
- You don't need to be at your desk to need an answer.
- You can make money without doing evil.
- There's always more information out there.
- The need for information crosses all borders.
- You can be serious without a suit.
- Great just isn't good enough.

Starbucks uses these brand values:

- Creating a culture of warmth and belonging, where everyone is welcome.
- Acting with courage, challenging the status quo and finding new ways to grow our company and each other.
- Being present, connecting with transparency, dignity and respect.
- Delivering our very best in all we do, holding ourselves accountable for results.

As you read through the brand values for each of these businesses, you'll notice they don't come as a surprise to you. Because these values are clearly communicated to employees and customers in everything they do. These values drive their corporate cultures, business operations, their marketing messages and visuals, the products they offer, and their philanthropic support.

Spend some time thinking about the core values for your business. Consider how these brand values tie into your brand story and your brand personality. Now, go to your strategy template and type up your brand values.

"One Liner"

Back in the day, tag lines were frequently used to attract people's attention using catchy phrases to help elicit emotion.

While tag lines still work for some businesses, I'm going to argue that your customers are less interested in how clever you can be with your words and more concerned about how well you can solve their problem.

What IS important to your customers is what you do. And frankly, answering that simple questions seems to be the one thing that brings businesses the most trouble.

In this section, we are going to work on cutting through the complicated explanations to get you to a clear, concise description of what problem you solve in a simple, relevant, repeatable way that your customers can quickly and easily understand.

Donald Miller writes extensively about "one-liners" in his book, "StoryBrand." According to Miller, your one-liner is a concise, compelling explanation that gets people interested in how you can help them.

If you've ever stumbled over yourself trying to explain to someone exactly what it is you do, you're going to love this simple exercise.

Your "one liner" needs to include three things:

1. The problem — What issues are making your customers uncomfortable? What is the major pain point they are trying to solve?

2. The solution — What product or service do you provide to take away the customer's pain or discomfort?

3. The benefit — What does the customer's life look like after you have solved their problem?

What are some of the most successful companies using as one-liners? Let's look at a few examples.

"We organize the world's information and make it universally accessible and useful."
~Google

"This is not a bed. This is proven quality sleep."
~Sleep Number Beds

"Escape to a World like no other. That's the power of magic."
~Disney Parks & Travel

Once you've answered the three basic questions, play with the words until you come up with a "one liner" that you feel comfortable with. It doesn't need to be cute, or witty, or clever. It just needs to be clear and concise.

Go ahead and document your one liner in your marketing strategy template.

We only have a split second to grab the attention of the right buyer. So the more quickly we can get our point across — what we do, who we do it for, and how they benefit — the more likely you are to get your prospects to linger and check you out.

Some places you should consider using your one liner in your marketing are:

- 10-second elevator pitch
- Intro sentence or headline on the home page of your website
- Intro sentence of your social media profiles
- E-mail signature
- Business cards

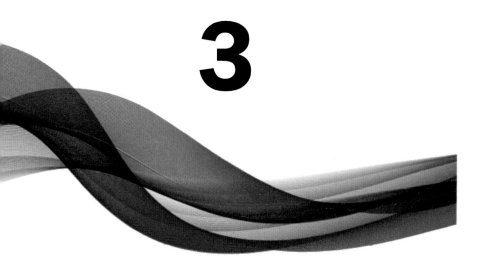

3

Know Your
AUDIENCE

You are NOT the hero of your story.

Let that sink in for a moment.

This is often difficult information for business owners to swallow. They picture themselves swooping in to save their customers from whatever problem they are plagued with.

But that "me" mentality will get you nowhere in a hurry.

I hate to be the bearer of bad news, but your customers could care less about you.

Your customers care about fulfilling their basic needs: physiology, safety, belonging, esteem, and self-actualization.*

Keeping these needs in mind as you get to know your audience helps you understand where you are on their spectrum of needs. The biggest mistake I see companies make when talking to their customer is to focus on the product or service they are selling.

If all of your marketing conversations revolve around you and what you are selling, you've probably lost the majority of your audience.

But how do you make the customer the hero and still sell them your stuff? And if the customer is the hero, what role do you play?

This is where we start to focus on a customer-centric marketing strategy. The customer is the center of your marketing plan. And to make them the hero, we need to get to know them as the main character of your story.

36

We need to know who they are, understand how they think, and get a sense of what needs drive them.

*Maslow's hierarchy of needs is a motivational theory in psychology outlining a five-tier model of human needs, often depicted as hierarchical levels within a pyramid.

Target Market

The sooner you come to the realization that not everyone is going to be your customer, the sooner you can get better at serving the ones who are.

Rather than wasting your time blanketing the market with generic messages that get heard by no one, define your target market so you can talk directly to a specific subset of people with a targeted message that's more likely to be seen and heard.

Not only will your messaging be more specific and clear, but your solutions and your business decisions will be more clear as well.

One of the easiest ways to define your target audience, is to take a look at who's already a customer and find commonalities or recurring themes.

There are three ways you can find information on your existing customers:

Direct Data — Just ask.

One of the best ways to get information about your customers is simply to ask them. You can survey your customers in all kinds of different ways.

You can send out an e-mail with a link to a survey. You can survey customers when they make purchases from you. Or you can ask customers questions when they contact your service department.

If you choose to survey your audience, be cognizant of their time and energy. Keep the survey short. Use as many yes/no and multiple choice questions as you can. The simpler, the better. If you can target your survey only to your best customers, they are going to be more likely to respond as they already feel a deeper connection to your brand.

What should you ask?

- If you don't already have demographic data on your customers, you will want to ask basic questions about age, gender, income, location, marital status, and education level.
- Ask them about their values, interests, hobbies, lifestyle, and behaviors. Be specific with these questions and frame them in a way that's quick and easy for your audience to answer.
- Find out what needs, challenges or frustrations they struggle with in relation to the product or service you offer.
- What is their decision making process when making a purchase?
- Where do they get their information? What media types do they frequently use?
- What do they find most useful about your product or service?

Indirect Data — Your business interacts with customers on a daily basis. So how can you capture those interactions and turn them into useful information you can use to learn more about your target audience?

First, you need to know where to look. Some of the common places businesses are finding data on their customers are:

- Website traffic
- Social media accounts
- Customer service interactions
- Sales interactions
- Purchase information

Having systems in place to track and analyze the data you gather from these mediums will help you get a better handle on who is buying your stuff, why they buy it, and how they are learning about you.

Third Party Data — If you don't have access to existing customer data or you're pivoting to a new market, you might be able to find free or paid information from government or non-profit sources or a data vendor to give you some insight into your target audience.

Using sources like the following often gives businesses a boost on defining their target audience when no information currently exists.

- U.S. Census Data (census.gov)
- Small Business Administration (SBA.gov)
- Pew Research Center
- Statista
- American Fact Finder
- Nielsen's MyBestSegments

Now that you have some information about your target audience, it's time to define it. Your ideal target audience will be the intersection between the ideal audience you want to work with and the audience who is most likely to buy from you.

There will be a certain set of people that you feel strongly about working with who may not necessarily be in a place to need your product. But there will also be a set of people who really want and need your product that you haven't necessarily considered. When we marry these two groups, you get a subset of people who you want to work with and who also want to work with you. Those are your people.

These are the people you should be marketing to directly. They are who you write to in your messaging, who you create for when you develop new offers, and who you make decisions for when creating products and services. That doesn't mean you won't still sell to the other two sets of people, it just means you are tailoring your message to the best, right fit.

Defining your target audience will help you:

- Narrow the focus of who you serve to better design your product, services, message, and pricing to their specific needs
- Understand the market so you can make rough predictions about sales and market share
- Know and understand your market intimately in order to make key decisions — like where you'll place your marketing dollars

Many businesses shy away from narrowing their potential audience. There's a fear that they might lose out on sales by not opening up their product to everybody. But the evidence shows that defining a specific niche increases your authority and allows you to create deeper personal connections with your target customer — which leads to more sales.

Tips for tackling your target audience:

- Consider the **demographics** of your target customer. Things like age, gender, location, income, education, marital status, education, revenue, # of employees, budget, etc.
- Think about **psychographic** details like personality, hobbies, attitude, interests, lifestyle, behavior, and niche.
- If your product has **competition**, who are the competitors targeting?
- If you have an existing product or service, what does your data say about your existing customers?

Now, open your strategy template and make a list of the characteristics of your target market — as many as you need.

Customer Need

Solving a problem is how businesses make sales. It's most likely what drove you to develop your business idea to begin with. You saw a need and created a solution. But honing in on the real customer need can be more difficult than it sounds.

When businesses are seeking new customers, too often they lead with their product or service. But remember, you are still NOT the hero of the conversation. If you spend all your energy pushing what you have to sell, your audience is going to drop like flies. Why? Because you are making it all about you — and that is boring and uninteresting.

Think about it. You're at a party and your friend introduces you to a guy they know. You shake hands and ask the guy to tell a little about himself. "I'm so glad you asked," he says. And he proceeds to drone on and on and on about how wonderful he is. He has fancy cars and an expensive education and a big house and a pretty wife and two brilliant kids and his business is making millions and his abs are flat and his hair is still its original natural color. Eventually, you excuse yourself to get another drink. You'll need one after that obvious display of narcissistic enthusiasm. Never once did he ask about you. Did he even ask your name?

Yawn...

Similarly, your customers don't want to hear you drone on an on about how wonderful you are. Realistically, they are mainly interested in what's in it for them. Once you capture their attention by telling them how great you can make them, they might be interested in hearing more about you.

You need to figure out what problem is keeping them up at night so you can lead with that solution right out of the gate – a solution that gets their attention.

Imagine this...

You're walking along, just minding your own business, barely keeping your eyes open....when, out of the blue, a sign pops up directly in front of you that says, "Come visit us at the sleep clinic. We have state of the art equipment and trained professionals." That's nice, you think. Good for you. And you keep walking.

Instead, imagine this...

You're walking along, just minding your own business, barely keeping your eyes open....when, out of the blue, a sign pops up directly in front of you that says, "Do you struggle to calm the thoughts racing through your head so you can get to sleep at night?" You gasp. It's like whoever sent this sign was in your head! How did they know how sleep deprived you are? How did they know your busy brain goes into overdrive every night at bedtime?
That second sign got your attention, didn't it? How powerful is it to understand your customers' struggles so

you can craft a message specifically for them?

Another common mistake I see businesses make is to assume they understand their customers' needs. But many times, even though they are still making steady sales, they find that customers are buying for a completely different reason.

So how do you know exactly what your customers' pain points are?

Just ask.

There is so much value in talking to your audience.

The age of technology makes it easy to connect with existing or potential customers. You can just flat out ask them what they struggle with. Put together a quick list of questions you can ask your current or potential customers that helps you understand some of their key challenges — both related and unrelated to your business.

Tips for tackling customer need:

- Pick a few of your top customers and invite them to hop on a quick call to answer a few questions.
- Conduct a survey using tools like SurveyMonkey, TypeForms, or Google Forms.
- Listen to your customers on social channels like Facebook, Twitter, Instagram LinkedIn, or other social platforms. What are you hearing? Do you find any recurring themes?
- Follow up a purchase or a customer interaction with a survey.

- Encourage reviews of your products and services.

Again, when you're talking to customers, always be considerate of their time. Be courteous, quick, and to the point. Here are some simple tips for effective interviews —
- Have pre-written questions ready so you are consistent and focused with your customers' time.
- Use yes/no or multiple choice questions as much as possible.
- Do a little background check on your interviewees. Make sure they fall into the criteria of your ideal customer.
- Keep your interview questions brief. Be conscientious of your interviewee's time.
- If you are meeting face-to-face or over the phone, be sure to LISTEN more than you talk.
- Always go out of your way to thank your participants for their time and the invaluable insight. Never incentivize the interview because you don't want to skew the results. But it's not a bad idea to send your interviewee a small token of appreciation once your interview is over.

It's a good idea to have a plan for your interview initiative. Feel free to jot down your answers to these questions in the notes section of your strategy template.

- Who will you connect with?
- How many interviews will you collect?
- What questions will you ask them?
- Where will you find your interviewees?
- What tool(s) will you use to collect your answers?

Once you've completed your interviews, analyze the responses and jot down your top customer need(s) in your strategy template.

Buyer Persona

A buyer persona is either a real or fictional representation of your ONE dream customer. It's a story painted for you and your team of a day in the life of that perfect person who you could work with a million times over if you had a chance.

I never like to play favorites, but if I was forced to pick a favorite section of this book, it would be the Buyer Persona.

Why?

Because creating buyer personas is the one exercise that takes many of my clients from offering a confusing array of disjointed services to becoming crystal clear on what their ideal customers look like, the major pain points their product or service addresses, the key messages that will bring in more leads and increase conversions, and where to find more people just like this.

A lot of businesses think, "Oh, but I already know who my ideal buyer is."

You might have a general idea who your ideal buyer is, but you are going to take that knowledge and go even deeper.

You are going to get into the mind of your ideal customer, explore their daily lives, and empathize with their struggles so you can have a richer understanding of how to speak to them, how to connect with them, and how to solve their issues. You are going to create the buyer's story.

Most businesses struggle with this exercise. As CEO, you are instinctively trained to think about making more sales. The thought of narrowing your ideal customer to one specific person can cause some to hyperventilate. But relax. You aren't really narrowing your audience, you are simply defining it, learning from it, and helping your team picture this person as they go about their day-to-day. It helps them think like your customer, be more customer-centric, and make smarter decisions.

The key to a meaningful buyer persona is to put a single face and name to the one person who — if you could — you would do business with over and over again. By visualizing this one person as your team goes through their day-to-day business tasks, they are helping to put the customer first and foremost in the decisions they make. And being a customer-centric business is key to your success.

Here are some tips for tackling your buyer persona:

- The best place to look to find your ideal buyer is your existing or past customers. Who was an absolute dream to work with? Who would work with a thousand times over? Who buys from you repeatedly and gives you raving reviews? You can even piece together an ideal buyer using a combination of several different customers.

- If you haven't found your exact ideal customer yet, you'll need to put your virtual goggles on and use your imagination. Maybe your ideal customer is even YOU?
- Creating a buyer persona is about humanizing your business processes. Find a picture of your ideal customer and plaster it on your planning documents and around your business. The idea is to have a picture in your mind at all times of WHO you are serving. It helps you consider things from your buyer's perspective.
- Force yourself to go beyond the surface. While it's important to know things about your buyer like their age, their zip code, their family size, etc., we want to consider what they're thinking, what they're feeling, their values, and their personality. We need to get inside their heads.

Use these guided questions to paint a vivid picture of your ideal buyer.

- What does a "day in the life" of your ideal buyer look like? Be as detailed as possible. Where does he work? What role does he play? What's his education level? What does his family look like? What does he do in his spare time? What books does he read? What music does he listen to? What shows does he watch on TV?
- What does your ideal buyer want to achieve in life? In business? In the short-term? In the long-term?
- What is your ideal buyer's main issue or pain point in relation to you business? Tell a story or draw a

verbal picture of how this issue impacts her life.
- Tell me about your ideal buyer's personal beliefs and values. How might that affect her buying process?
- If your item is a higher ticket item, talk about how your ideal buyer manages the expense. Does she create a budget? Save her money? Get a loan? Charge it to a credit card? Make payments? How does this big ticket purchase impact her from a financial perspective? Will it make things tight for her family for a period of time? Will she even even blink at the expense?
- Where does your ideal buyer hang out? Where is her social circle? Does she have a business or networking circle? Is she online? Where specifically? What does she do there? Does her personal online social activity look different from her professional online social activity? When she is online, where is she spending her time? What is she reading, searching, scrolling? When she's not online, what does she spend her social time doing?

As you think about these questions and how they pertain to your ideal buyer, begin creating a story in your mind. Your buyer's story helps you connect to him or her on a personal level so you can more easily visualize them as you make decisions about your products, services, marketing, and message.

As you create this buyer persona, remember the key elements of a good story:

The Character — paint a picture of your buyer. Who are they? Give enough information about the buyer that you and your team can easily visualize them.

The Setting — what is the environment that your buyer lives in? What are they surrounded with?

The Plot — what is the buyer's story?

The Problem — what does the buyer struggle with? What keeps them up at night?

The Guide — who are the people or tools the buyer relies on for support, for guidance, or for information?

The Resolution — what does the buyer's life look like once the problem has been solved? What goals have they achieved?

Write this story in your strategy template.

4

Validate Your Idea

You can have the most unique idea in the world, but if no one is willing to pay for it, you have no business. Are you solving a big enough problem to sustain your business year over year?

Validating an idea isn't important only at the beginning of business. Sales can dry up at any moment. Regularly reviewing the market opportunity for what you have to sell will not only allow you to make projections about your sales and revenue volume, but will also help you stay on top of trends that could keep you ahead of the curve when it comes to developing new products and services.

In this chapter, you will discover strategies for staying ahead of changing market conditions and methods for calculating potential market opportunity.

Market Opportunity

Understanding market opportunity can have a profound effect on your business.

Successful CEOs are looking at market opportunity to:

- Create long-term sales and revenue forecasts
- Secure financing or venture capital
- Provide insight for product and service development

There is no exact science for calculating market opportunity, but here are some tips for tackling your market opportunity.

Total Market Audience

First, you need to identify the total size of your market. In a recent chapter, you narrowed your target audience using demographics and psychographics. Now try to quantify that market to help you understand the size and opportunity for your business.

Finding the total size of your audience is messy business. There is no exact science. But you can make some close guesstimates using tools such as:

- Small Business Administration (www.SBA.gov),
- U.S. Census Bureau
- FedStats.gov
- EconomicIndicators.gov
- Purchased data from 3rd party provider

Another way to estimate an audience size is to calculate how many people are buying something similar from your competitors. You might be able to pull this information from third-party data providers that collect information on audiences in your industry.

Where are other places your target audience can be found?

- Associations
- Clubs
- Licenses
- Memberships
- Groups
- Subscriptions
- Complementary products or services they buy

Document your different audience segments and totals in your marketing strategy document.

Market Penetration

The total size of your audience is not a good indicator of how many people are likely to buy from you.

Some industry experts project that only 2%-6% of your audience, if you are marketing to consumers, are buyers of your product or service and 10%-20% if you are selling to other businesses.

There are other factors that impact your market penetration. If your product is necessary or mandated, your penetration rate will be higher. If your product is highly specialized, expect your penetration rate to be lower.

Calculate your market penetration:

> Total target market x market penetration rate = estimated market size

Document your calculation in your marketing strategy template.

Market Share

You aren't quite done yet. Now that you know the estimated size of the market — the people who are most likely to be open to what you have to offer — you need to set a goal or make an estimate for what percentage of that market you plan to turn into customers.

This is where a little more fancy guess work comes in handy.

What percentage of this market can you capture and turn into customers? What percentage of this market will *realistically* become your customer?

Earlier, you set some pretty lofty goals for yourself. At least one of those goals most likely involved revenue or sales. This calculation will help you visualize how much effort it will take to achieve those goals.

Estimated market size x forecasted market share = # of customers

If there is more competition in your market, your forecasted market share will probably be lower than where there is little to no competition. Other factors that can affect market share are:

- The quality of your product or service offering
- The amount of marketing you do
- Customer service
- Customer experience

These factors will either positively or negatively affect referrals, customer loyalty, and customer acquisition. Document this calculation in your marketing strategy template.

Revenue Forecast

If you know the number of customers you anticipate serving over the next 3-5 years, you can predict how much revenue you will be able to bring in to your business.
For this calculation, it's helpful to know, on average, how much your customers spend with you. If you have it, you can use your Customer Lifetime Value (CLV is the average of revenue you make from one customer over the course of their relationship with you), or average purchase amount.

> # of customers x average customer spend = forecasted revenue

Now that you have these calculations, you can start to make more predictions:

- How much revenue will you bring in on an annual basis? Monthly?
- At what rate do you plan to grow the business?
- What will your profit margins look like?
- Does your forecasted revenue include repeat business or one-time purchases?

Document this calculation in your marketing strategy template.

Now, go back to the goals you set in chapter 1. Do you need to make any changes based on this information?

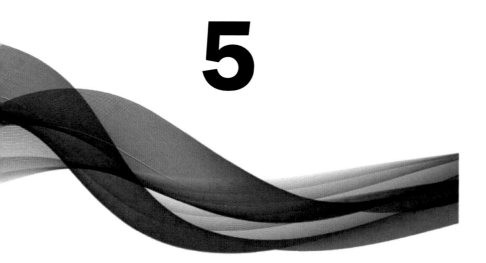

5

Stand Out

Back in the 1970's (before many of you were even born), consumers were exposed to an average of 500 advertising messages a day. They were being marketed to in places like TV, newspapers, radio, billboards, and in-store displays. The world of advertising really took off.

If that seems overwhelming, consider the nearly 5,000 messages your customers are now seeing each and every day. Pretty much if you can see it or hear it, there's probably an ad on it. Advertisers are clamoring for attention — and your customers have hit sensory overload.

So how do you compete for your ideal customer's attention amidst all the other messages?

As actor Steve Martin once said, "Be so good they can't ignore you."

You need to offer something unique — something that no one else is offering — and then make it all about what's important to your customer.

To figure out what makes you unique, start by knowing what's out there.

Direct Competition

In order to figure out what sets you apart, you need to know how you stack up.

Every time your customers get ready to make a purchase, they are presented with choices. There are probably many other businesses offering similar products or services. When your customers get ready to buy, they have to make a decision whether they will buy from you or from one of your competitors.

Any business who sells a product or service that is similar to what you offer is called a direct competitor. Direct competitors are typically what business owners think of when they consider their competition.

> Ex: Imagine you are a fleece clothing manufacturer. Your customers get cold and and they need something to help them keep warm during the winter months. You sell a fleece jacket. There are several other fleece manufacturers that also sell jackets.
>
> These are your direct competitors.

In this section, focus on your top 3 competitors. Go ahead and list them in your strategy template.

For each of your three competitors, assess how they are doing business in order to understand what factors your customers consider when they are presented with different options.

Tips for tackling your direct competitor analysis:

- For this exercise, focus only on your top three competitors. While you can (and should) conduct a more comprehensive analysis of your competition if you have the resources to do so, it can be distracting and overwhelming.
- DO use free information to study your competition. Websites, brochures, social media accounts, Google, and paid ads are great tools for seeing what they are up to.
- DO reach out to your target audience to ask questions about your competition.
- Do secret shop your competitors.

Here is what you need to find out about your competition:

- What target market do they serve?
- Where are they doing business?
- How long have they been in business?
- What size are they (employees, revenue, sales, etc)?
- What products and/ or services does this competitor offer?
- How do they price their offerings?
- What does this competitor do well?
- What do they struggle with?
- What do you do better?
- Where are you not as good?
- Describe the competitor's marketing efforts.
- What is their key message?
- How do they primarily market to customers?

- Why do their customers choose them?
- Why do your customers choose you over the competitor?
- How is their customer experience?
- What do their customer reviews say?

Answer these questions for each of your top 3 direct competitors and document your findings in your strategy template.

This research may seem tedious, but it's so important when it comes to knowing how you standing out.

Indirect Competition

Not only are your customers presented with various options from competitors offering the same or similar solutions as you, they also have the option of choosing from a variety of different offers that still solve their main problem.

> Ex: You are still a fleece clothing manufacturer. Your customers still get cold in the winter months and need something to help keep them warm. They could buy a fleece jacket from you. Or, they could buy a down vest, a sweater, cardigan or a sweatshirt that also keeps them warm during the cold of winter.

> These are your indirect competitors. They are still solving your customers' problem (keeping warm), but doing it with a different approach.

Tips for tackling your indirect competitor analysis:

- For this exercise, focus on as many of your indirect competitors as you need.
- DO use free information to study your competition. Websites, brochures, social media accounts,

Google, and paid ads are great tools for seeing what they are up to.

- DO reach out to your target audience to ask questions about your competition.
- DO secret shop your competitors.
- DO NOT spend as much time digging into your indirect competition as your direct competition.

Here is what you need to find out about your competition:

- What target market do they serve?
- Where are they doing business?
- How long have they been in business?
- What products and/or services does this competitor offer?
- How do they price their offerings?
- What does this competitor do well?
- What do they struggle with?
- What do you do better?
- Where are you not as good?
- What is their key message?
- Why do their customers choose them?
- Why do your customers choose you over the competitor?

Document your indirect competitor analysis in your strategy template.

Another source of indirect competition that is worth a mention is called **alternative product or service** and is completely unrelated to your offering, but often competes for your customers' dollars.

Ex: You still manufacture fleece clothing. Your customers are still cold in the winter months. But rather than buying a warm jacket, they might choose to spend their money on a cozy blanket or a space heater instead.

61

Consider alternative products and services your customers might choose. List them in your strategy template.

And finally, what about the customers that choose to do nothing?

Doing nothing — making no purchases — is also an option. What happens to your customers who choose to ride out their problem and make no changes? What does their life look like continuing with the status quo?

Document this in your strategy template.

Often I find that clients who have a handle on their competition spend too much time trying to copy every move they make. While they think it's helping them stay competitive, it's actually counterproductive. Your competitors have a different business than you. By taking your focus away from your vision to keep up with their business, you lose sight of your own goals and set your team back from achieving what you set out to achieve.

Stay in your own lane. There is strength in sticking to what you do best. Focus, instead, on what you do differently and why.

The key to using a competitive analysis in a productive way is to understand what drives customers to buy and why. Your goal is not necessarily to "steal" customers from your competitor, but to better understand what attracts your customers to you versus your competition.

Once you find that thing that you do differently — that makes your customers choose you — find a way to leverage that thing in your marketing and customer communications.

Unique Selling Proposition

How saturated is your market?

In a saturated market, there is a lot of competition for your customers' business. It's much harder to compete and more emphasis needs to be placed on finding the thing that sets you apart. If you are in a saturated market, adding value for your customers will be key.

"...instead of focusing on beating the competition, you focus on making the competition irrelevant by creating a leap in value for buyers and your company, thereby opening up new and uncontested market space."
~W. Chan Kim, Blue Ocean Strategy

Use your competitive analysis to help you identify the uniqueness that adds that leap in value for your customers. In a nutshell, why is your product or service different or better than other similar solutions in the marketplace?

In our current economy, barriers to entry are low and unique new products and ideas are really hard to come by. If you think you have a brand new idea, chances are somebody else is already doing it. That's the nature of the free market.

So how do you compete?

Since having the best product or service is no longer enough, you need to figure out what gaps your competitors have left for you to fill. To find these gaps, have a knowledgable grasp on your industry, your competition, and your customer.

Here are some tips for tackling your unique selling proposition:

- Review your competitive analyses. Who is your competition? What do they do well and what do you do better?
- Review your customer need. What issues is your target audience faced with? How do you address these issues? How do your competitors address these issues? Are there any gaps?
- Ask your existing or ideal customers what draws them to you vs. the competition.
- What does your one-liner say about your business?

In order to be effective, a unique selling proposition needs to focus on the *one* thing you do differently or better than anyone else. Many times, during this exercise, clients will come to me with a list of 3-5 things they think is unique about their business. And while it's possible to have these key differentiators, it won't have much impact unless you focus on the *most important* differentiator.

Consider Zappos, for instance. Zappos is an online store specializing in shoes. There are many online shoe companies to choose from. But what sets Zappos apart from other online shoe stores is free returns. This key differentiator allows Zappos to market to people who value the flexibility of purchasing online without incurring fees when something doesn't work for them. And because of this unique selling proposition, Zappos is able to command premium prices for their products.

Think about your company's key differentiator and document your unique selling proposition in your strategy template.

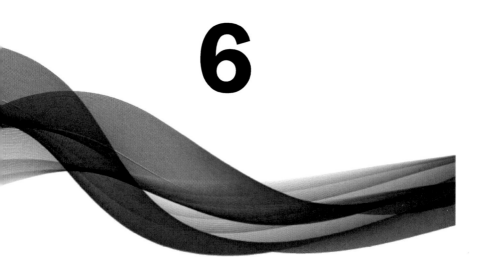

6

Wow Your Customers

Your business is in existence because you recognized a gap — a problem that somebody somewhere struggled with — and you found a way to solve it. But simply solving a problem isn't enough to guarantee a successful business.

These three fundamentals of creating a solution to a problem will determine the opportunity for success in your business.

Do you solve a big enough problem?

The world is plagued with struggles. Every day, people are inconvenienced, overwhelmed, short on time, short on money, and just plain exhausted. There are any number of opportunities out there to help people regain time, money, control, or happiness. But are they willing to pay for it?

Years ago, Coca-Cola announced a change to their main drink recipe. They called it New Coke. Their customers were outraged. Why? Because they liked the recipe just the way it was. There was no NEED to update the recipe when the old one satisfied people's sweet tooth just fine. The company eventually ended up bringing back the original recipe, calling it Coke Classic and the New Coke simply fell off.

The problem you solve needs to be painful enough for your customers that they are ready and willing to throw money at you to fix it. In other words, how valuable is your solution to your customers?

How well do you solve the problem?

Your solution needs to be thoughtful and well-designed. If your customers fix one problem only to trade it for another, that's a turn off that will bring you bad reviews and lost business.

Wow! Chips, for example, were made with an ingredient called olestra — which gave the chips the same amazing flavor and texture but without all the fat. People were clamoring to buy this product so they could eat their junk food guilt free. Unfortunately, Olestra also turned out to be a fantastic laxative and this product was a flop. Customers were trading one problem (getting fat from eating junk food) for another problem (racing to the bathroom).

Delivering on what you promised is key to customer satisfaction. Do what you say you are going to do and do it well.

How many people have that problem?

When we discussed market opportunity in chapter 4, you did some calculations to estimate the number of people likely to become your customer. Review those numbers.

How accurate do you think those numbers are? Are there enough people who have this problem to warrant your time and effort to create and sell a solution? Will you be able to find those people who have this specific problem? It's not uncommon for businesses to continue iterating their products and services as they grow, improve, and get feedback from customers.

Assuming you have a marketable product or service idea, let's dive into maximizing its value for your customers.

Define Your Product or Service

Bear with me in this section. The work may seem tedious to you, but it's critical that your team — current and future — have a clear picture of exactly what it is you are selling.

Your products or services are your source of revenue. It's important to give them attention when considering your marketing strategy. And remember, you are creating this strategy not only for yourself, but for anyone you bring on board to support your vision.

So capturing these details in writing not only saves you and your team from repeating this information over and over, but gives you a birds-eye view of what and how your customers view what you offer. You may see opportunities for change.

Here are some tips for tackling your product definition:

Define or outline the following information about each product or service (or type of product or service) you offer.

- What is the name of the product or service?
- We've already mentioned it, but what is the customer need your product satisfies?
- What is your specific solution? Describe your product and its features here.
- If you have a tangible product, what kind of variety do you offer? Do you offer different sizes, colors, or formats?
- If you have a tangible product, what kind of packaging does your product use?
- How will your customer use it?
- Where will they use it?
- If you are offering a tangible product, does it have options (color, size, etc)?
- What price are you charging?
- Where is your price set in relation to your competition?
- Why did you set your price there?
- What does it cost to produce and maintain your offering?
- How will your customers find your product?

- Does your product or service come with any kind of guarantee, warranty, money-back period or additional service?

Create A Customer Journey

Your customer's journey starts the minute they first come in contact with you. It's the story your customers experience with your brand from the initial introduction through their (hopefully) long-term relationship with you.

Like any good story, there's always a hero, a villain, and a guide. As Donald Miller describes in his book, "StoryBrand," your customer's journey is about YOU guiding them into hero status by helping them defeat the villain.

You do that by anticipating where your customer is at in their journey and present them with the right tools and action steps to GUIDE them into the next phase of the buying process.

While it may not appear on the surface, a customer journey can be quite complex. Your job is to take this complex journey and make it appear as streamlined and simple as possible for your customer.

Some refer to this journey as a funnel. A marketing (or sales) funnel works just like it sounds. You bring in as many leads as possible through the top, and it funnels them down into a purchase. At each phase of a funnel, people drop out until you are left with the ones who actually purchase. It looks something like this:

Funnels are a huge marketing buzz word. Multiple software systems have been built to digitally support this aspect of your marketing. Businesses are building funnels to maximizing sales. Agencies are selling plug-and-play templates. And these templates do work.

But the drawback of this approach is that it is focused on increasing sales, maximizing exposure, and driving more activity. Where is your customer in this process? They are being "funneled" along a conveyer belt and are at risk of being turned off by "sleazy sales" tactics and feeling "tricked" into buying.

Another drawback of the marketing funnel is that it typically stops at the point the buyer makes a purchase.

What about repeat purchases and customer loyalty?

A customer journey, on the other hand, places the customer at the center the story. Instead of putting your customers on your conveyer belt of templated clicks and e-mails, look instead at the places your customers are most likely to interact with your brand and craft an experience around that journey. Find what they are needing most to advance to the next stage of their buying decision and provide it to them in a way that meets them where they are. The customer journey doesn't end at purchase. It's tracked all the way through the relationship with your brand so you can understand repeat purchase needs and behaviors and nurture customer loyalty.

| AWARENESS | CONSIDERATION | DECISION | PURCHASE | POST-PURCHASE | LOYALTY | ADVOCACY |

Perhaps one of the biggest benefits of focusing on a customer journey is your ability to focus the work on the things that matter most in your business.

While the concept of a marketing funnel and a customer journey are fairly similar, the key difference is in the perspective. One is created from the perspective of the brand with the purpose of driving more sales. The other is created from the perspective of the customer with the purpose of serving and building relationships.

Let's take another look at that customer journey graphic and review the different stages of the customer buying process.

- Awareness — someone encounters your brand and becomes aware of its existence.
- Consideration — the buyer has become committed to solving an issue and is evaluating all the available options
- Decision — the buyer has decided on a specific type of solution and is comparing each provider
- Purchase — the buyer commits to a specific solution
- Post-purchase — delivery of the solution and buyer adoption
- Loyalty — buyer considers purchasing another of the same solution or expanding to another type of solution you offer
- Advocacy — becomes a loyal buyer and actively shares their positive experience with others

Tips for tackling your customer journey:

We are going to map out a customer journey for each of the types of products or services you sell. Try to capture as best you can (using actual data or anecdotal information) what your ideal buyer needs during each stage of the buyer journey.

Other questions to consider as you think through the buyer journey:

- When does your ideal buyer realize they have a problem? Is it something that causes them great issue? Does your ideal buyer even realize they

have a problem? Is this something on which you will need to educate them?
- Once your buyer decides to address the problem, how and where does he begin his search for the solution?
- How does she evaluate her options?
- What criteria does he use to select a solution?
- What will your ideal buyer consider an influence during the decision-making process?
- Are there others who are involved in the purchase decision?
- Who does she seek referrals from?
- Does he consider testimonies? Who does he trust?
- What does she rely on to determine if her purchase is a good idea?

Use this information to place yourself where your customers are likely to be hanging out during each stage of the buying process.

Awareness

The awareness stage is all about connecting with new potential customers. During the awareness stage, consider all the different ways a potential customer might become aware of your brand and make a list.

Some examples of tools you can use in the awareness stage: paid advertising, free press, referrals, speaking engagements, events, direct mail, search engines, partnerships, social shares, branding.

When the buyer first comes in contact with you, how aware are they of their problem? Many times, buyers may not even realize they have an issue until they are introduced to something that makes their life better. Whether or not prospects realize they have an issue will impact they types of activity you focus on during the awareness stage.

In our customer centric model, we want to look back at the buyer persona we created. Consider the ways that your ideal buyer is most likely to come in contact with you. Focus on making those specific channels highly effective.

If most people are not yet aware of their problem, think about what answers, resources, education, research data, opinions, and insight they might be looking for. Where do you think they would look for that information? How do they prefer to consume it?

Consideration
During the consideration stage, the prospect is aware of their problem and is "considering," or evaluating, their different options. They may be in this stage for quite a long time, or they may breeze through this stage in a matter of minutes. Your goal, during this stage, is to demonstrate why your solutions is (or in some cases, is not) a good fit.

The consideration stage is sometimes referred to as "nurturing" your leads. You'll be focused on connecting and relationship building.

Some examples of tools you can use during the consideration stage: guides, seminars, white papers, case studies, brochures, demonstrations, webinars, trials, audits, videos, comparisons, e-mail campaigns, consultations

As you are building the relationship, remember to be helpful and provide value.

Depending on your situation, the consideration stage may be broken into smaller sub-stages. If your ideal customer has a lengthier buying process, the more sub-stages you need to consider. The key is to understand the customer journey and to provide the right tools at the right point in their decision-making process.

Decision

The prospect is ready to buy. This is a critical stage in the buyer's journey. They are ready to make their choice. They are ready to open up their wallets and spend money. Will they spend it with you?

Some examples of tools you can use in the decision stage: a simple offer, testimonials, pricing, special discounts, and proposals.

At this stage, the buyer may have narrowed their choice to a couple of different options. So present the prospect with information and tools that help them differentiate you from the competition and determine if you are the best fit.

Purchase

Your job, at this stage of the buying process, is to make it incredibly simple for the prospect to choose you. If the purchase process is complicated, confusing, or takes too much effort on the part of the buyer they may choose another option.

Some examples of things you can do to simplify the purchase stage:

- Offer online purchasing
- Accept multiple forms of payment
- Online signatures on quotes, proposals, and contracts
- Offer customer service

- Provide a phone number
- Remove unnecessary steps
- Use digital tools for collaborating
- Fast web speed
- Secure payment processing

Many "marketing funnels" stop at the point of purchase. But if you are truly capturing your customer's entire journey, you need to also consider what happens AFTER the purchase.

Instead of looking like a funnel, your customer journey ends up looking more like an hour glass.

At the beginning of the journey, you are filtering prospects from awareness into purchase. But after the purchase, your goal is to spread awareness as your happy customers refer you to other potential buyers.

Post-Purchase

The experience your customer has immediately following their purchase is probably the most critical point in their journey. This is your opportunity to shine — to prove to your customer that they made a great purchase decision. Poor post-purchase experiences result in lost revenue through returns, bad reviews, and negative publicity. Think about what type of support buyers might need from you once they've placed their order. Will they need extra help between the time they've purchased and the time they receive their products or services? What about once the the product arrives? Or once their service begins?

Some examples of tools you can use to boost your customers' post-purchase experience: order confirmation, tracking orders/shipping, communicating next steps, easily accessible customer support, manuals, demos, how-to videos, welcome messages, checklists, kick-off meetings, training, and return process.

Think about ease and simplicity. If your customers have to hunt these things down, their experience with you could use some improvement. And that feedback will come back to you in less than 5-star reviews. Anticipate your customer's needs and make those resources available with little effort on your customer's part.

Loyalty
In general, it costs almost five times more money to attract new customers than to keep the existing ones. Yet the majority of businesses put most of their efforts into new acquisition rather than retention.

In the Loyalty phase, the focus is on nurturing the customers you already have. They need your help getting to 100% adoption of the product or service they purchased. And ultimately, we want them to feel confident enough in their experience to purchase from us again.

Some examples of tools you can use to boost customer loyalty: customer community, usage tips or tricks, product or service updates, customer loyalty program, follow up, rewards, customer service, reviews, surveys, personalized connections, product upgrades, up-sells, lateral sales, and transparency. Nurturing customers can be as simple as positive engagement. Find ways to connect with your customers that make them feel valued and supported.

Advocacy

For most businesses, advocacy is the most desired outcome of a customer relationship. When a customer recommends you to their circle, that's not only free advertising for you, but people are more likely to make a purchase from a brand that's been recommended by someone they already know, like, and trust.

Some examples of tools you can use to encourage customer advocacy: ask for testimonials, ask for referrals, ask them to be a reference, special invitations, product previews, ask them to serve on an advisory board, affiliate program, influencer program, special group membership, gifts, feature them in your marketing.

At this stage, your job is to lift up the customers who sing your praises, enfold them into your "family," and ensure they continue to remain a raving fan. Find ways to make them feel involved in your mission and vision. Make it easy and rewarding for them to continue to share the love with others.

There is no exact template for a marketing funnel. These stages of the buying process are just suggestions for you to consider as you map out the buyer's journey. The information is meant to be a guide as you consider your unique customer and your unique situation.

Mapping a buyer's journey may seem a little overwhelming. I've created a handy template in Trello to simplify the process. Visit www.caseygromervmo.com/resources to download your template and a quick training video.

7

Putting It All Together

Congratulations! We have spent some major time in this book hammering out the foundations of your business. You now have a written tool you can use as a guide for making important decisions, on-boarding new employees, prioritizing marketing initiatives, and creating a messaging platform.

But just having a document capturing the strategic foundations of your business is not enough. Now you need to understand how to use it in your day-to-day business.

First, this document is not meant to be your company's

best kept secret. Your strategic marketing plan should be printed out and re-visited ideally once a quarter. A quick review with your leadership team will allow you to address any tweaks that need to be made or re-focus you if you find yourself veering too far from the path.

Next, share this information with your teams. I don't just mean provide them a copy of the document (although you certainly could). But find ways to incorporate your mission and vision into daily life at your company. Talk about these foundations during employee meetings. Use this information to on-board new employees and contractors. Get your team on the same page working toward the same outcomes.

But your strategic marketing plan alone is not enough to get you out of the day-to-day so you can focus on being CEO.

You need marketing systems for planning, managing people, and directing the work. I'm about to implode all of your bad habits, your pieced-together campaigns, and your shoot from the hip methodology.

Here's where you need to roll up your sleeves and get to work.

Plan Your Strategic Marketing Objectives

One of the biggest marketing mistakes I see businesses make is focusing too hard on short-term gains and not enough on the end game. They push the boundaries on

ROI, trying to eek out as much performance as they can from their marketing spend.

But what results is low quality campaigns, poor results, and wasted money. There is a time and place for this type of marketing, but it shouldn't be your overarching strategy. Instead, visualize where your company is headed so you can map out what needs to happen to get there. Once you start breaking those steps into more digestible chunks, you'll be able to articulate a clear marketing plan of action that's focused and realistic. I guarantee you will get more bang for your buck over the long-term with this approach than using the mad dash for cash methods many businesses choose.

There are 5 major levers you can pull in your marketing to impact revenue and growth:

- Product
- Price
- Place
- Promotion
- People

Let's explore how we can use these areas of marketing to impact the bottom line.

Product (or Service) — It surprises many people when they learn product is actually a piece of marketing. If you want make a change to your bottom line, take a look at what you offer. Are there improvements you can make to your existing products or services? Are there new products or services you could offer? Is there anything that's not performing that you can eliminate from your offering?

Price — An obvious lever and one that most companies gravitate to first. Any fluctuation in price is going to have an impact on sales. In most cases, this price change is seen in terms of sales, discounts, and coupons. But changing price could possibly mean a price increase as well.

Place — Keeping with the "P" theme, place refers to the distribution of your product or service. Where are your customers buying your stuff? And are there new channels of distribution you should consider or eliminate?

Promotion — The most common marketing lever is promotion. What types of marketing and advertising activity will you use to promote what you're selling?

People — This lever is often forgotten. There are two ways we can use people to change the bottom line in our business. The first (and more obvious way) is to consider your audience. Should you niche? Expand into a new target market?

But people also refers to the people you surround yourself with as CEO of your business. Marketing is a high dollar activity and is highly scrutinized for ROI. Part of your responsibility as CEO is to make sure you have the RIGHT people on your team to carry you forward. Are there people you could add to the marketing team to bring value? People who aren't a good fit you could let go?

Once you've stacked your marketing team, make sure

you continue to nurture those resources. If they believe in your mission, if they feel valued and supported, they will show up every day giving you 100%. How can you invest in the resources you already have? Are there training opportunities? Team building exercises? Meetings? Gifts? Bonuses? Encouragement?

I have a system for planning and prioritizing these annual strategic marketing objectives. And I'm happy to share the template and a quick video walk-through with you. Visit www.caseygromervmo.com/resources to download it.

Set A Marketing Budget

Asking companies to set aside a budget for marketing is almost like asking my 8-year old to clean her room. She knows it needs to get done, but she keeps dragging it out because it's boring and overwhelming and she doesn't know where to start.

Likewise, many visionary business owners cringe at the word "budget." And I'm guessing one of the first things you outsourced in your business had to do with your finances. Perhaps someone is keeping your books, doing your taxes, or maybe you have a trusted CFO.

Finance people are great! And one of the things I would encourage is to get your finance team and your marketing team to talk. Because often times, finance people see marketing as an expense. And marketing people see finance people as dream squashers. Okay, not really. But maybe just a little.

The finance people want to help you maximize your profit, decrease your expenses, and grow the financial health of your business. They won't mind spending money on marketing if they are comfortable that marketing is going to result in a return on your investment. What finance people don't always understand is that not all marketing spend is going to result in an immediate boost in revenue. That would be dreamy, but it just doesn't happen that way. And the reality is, without marketing, you have no business.

So a great compromise is to get your finance people and your marketing people in the same room and create a compromise. That compromise is a budget. Setting parameters for your annual and quarterly spending lends a level of comfort to the finance team and gives marketing folks a set of boundaries within which they need to perform.

Before you sit down to create your budget, have some historical information handy. How much have you traditionally spent on marketing? What did you spend last quarter? What did you spend last year? What percentage of your annual net revenue is that number?

Most businesses spend anywhere from 5%-30% of their annual net revenue on marketing. Where you fall in this continuum depends on your industry and your capacity for growth. The lower end of the budget range is typically for businesses who want or need to do the bare minimum.

The upper end of the budget range is for businesses who are hungry for growth. It's important to remember that the upper end of this range can be a hefty sum of money. And if you have a lot of overhead, you'll want to make sure you can sustain this spend knowing you may not get an immediate return on this investment.

If you aren't sure where you fall, start with roughly 10%-15% of your net annual revenue.

The wonderful thing about this method of budgeting is that it grows as you grow. So the more you make, the more you have to spend. You are never locked in at a certain percentage of spend. One year, you may have stretch goals you need to meet so you spend more. The next year you might choose to spend less.

There is a very simple template I use for planning quarterly budgets. And I'm happy to share the template and a quick video walk-through with you. Visit www.caseygromervmo.com/resources to get access.

Your Marketing Dashboard

In the last section, we covered a delicate topic: Marketing as an expense.

If your marketing isn't performing for you — if you are

spending money and not seeing results — then it's just an expense. But if your marketing is growing your business, then it's an investment. And just as with any investment, it may take time before you realize your return.

So how can you tell if your marketing is working for you?

In this section, we are going to talk about defining key performance indicators and tracking your marketing efforts.

Key Performance Indicators (KPI's) are basically a measurement of how well your business is meeting its objectives. As CEO, it's your job to keep an eye on these KPIs so you can step in and provide direction or guidance if things appear to be veering off track.

At the CEO level, I encourage my clients to select 10-12 (no more than 15) KPIs that are the best reflection of the growth of the business. If you look back at the long-term goals you set for your company back in chapter 1, you have your first set of 3-5 KPIs. Your goals define your idea of success and provide a specific and measurable path towards achieving your vision.

Each business's definition of success is different, so there is no perfect formula for tracking KPIs. However, there are some commonly used KPIs that you might want to consider.

Here are some tips for tackling your KPIs:

- Revenue

- Sales
- Profit
- Growth rate
- Customer satisfaction
- Employee engagement

While the above KPIs are heavily impacted by marketing, they represent the performance of your entire company. And that is what you, as the CEO, should be most concerned with.

But there are many more KPIs that could (and should) be tracked to ensure the health of your business. Each team should operate under their own set of KPIs. Here are some examples of KPIs your marketing team may be held accountable for:

- Traffic
- Leads
- Conversion rates
- Cost per acquisition
- Customer lifetime value
- Retention rate
- Customer engagement

There are hundreds more examples of specific KPIs you can track, which is why many CEOs get lost in the "data jungle."

Your dashboard should highlight only the top 10-12 (or less) measurements that give you a snapshot of the health of your company or your marketing.

I also want to take a minute to encourage you to hold your team accountable for tracking the success of any marketing efforts. Before you spend money on your marketing, understand exactly what you need that marketing to do for you and set some parameters. If your marketing (or your team) isn't performing, it's a clear indicator that something needs to stop or change.

8

Your Marketing In Action

So far, we've talked a lot about your marketing foundation. We spent some time setting up your planning and execution processes. But what we haven't covered is who is doing the work.

Because it should not be you.

In order for you to truly step into your role as CEO of your business, you have to get comfortable handing over the marketing of your business to someone you trust — someone who will be in charge of the strategy, the planning, the execution, performance tracking, hiring, firing, making decisions, handling crises, and making sure stuff gets done. You can't handle it all on your own and still be the visionary your team (and your business) needs you to be.

It's time to start staffing your team.

If you've taken the time to incorporate the philosophies of this book into your business, you should now have a marketing strategy and supporting systems and processes that make it easy for you to hand over to an expert who can support you in your vision. Think of this person as your Chief Marketing Officer, your Marketing Director, or your Marketing Integrator. Whatever you call this person, consider them part of your leadership team — a partner you can leverage to spread your mission and vision to the world.

Ideally, you are surrounded with a team of these experts — each with their own specialized skill set. Each of these supporting roles has one goal in mind — to help you translate your vision and turn your dreams into action.

Your leadership team:

Your marketing team:

9

Marketing Growth Formula Resources

If the formulas in this book appealed to you, and you would like help implementing these strategies and systems in your own business so you can truly flourish in your role as CEO, you can visit us at www. caseygromervmo.com/work-with-me to learn more about the following services:

Marketing Growth Formula

Phase I
You wouldn't build a house without understanding how all the pieces of the home need to come together to work for the customer — the people who will live there. You'd start with a blueprint.

Similarly, you need a blueprint for your business. Every decision you make is based on the guiding principles you've established in your blueprint — your strategy.

Your blueprint is a guide for your team. It aligns them towards the same mission and goals and provides them with guidelines for executing on your vision.

Phase II
If the blueprint establishes the foundation of your business, the roadmap provides the path to getting there.

During this phase, we will work on setting up your marketing systems that allow you to plan and prioritize your work. With your roadmap in place, your team will be focused on the marketing activities that are most critical for your growth.

The systems we develop in The Roadmap grows with your business and can be repeated for each planning period.

Phase III
WHO you surround yourself with in your business is as important to executing your vision as what they do.

Finding talented people you can trust who are a good fit for your business, fit your budget, and have skills in the right areas is challenging and time consuming.

As we build your team, I will stack your team with just the people you need to help you get *ish* done.

Phase IV
The whole idea of stepping into your role as CEO and visionary is to get yourself out of the day-to-day details so you can focus on the big picture of growing your business

In this phase, a trusted professional will optimize your company's marketing activity, keep your team accountable, and systematize the day-to-day management of your teams so you don't have to.

VIP Days
If time is of the essence, then ask about Marketing Growth Formula 1- and 2-day VIP sessions.

Strategy Calls
Does your marketing need a quick tweak? In 60-minutes, we can work through any of the concepts presented in *Marketing Growth Formula*.